GU00870722

Enjoy!

KITCHEN CALM

Kitchen Calm

Dermot O'Flynn

CURRACH
PRESS

First published in 2005 by
CURRACH PRESS
55A Spruce Avenue, Stillorgan Industrial Park, Blackrock,
Co Dublin, Ireland

www.currach.ie
www.kitchencalm.com
kitchencalm@eircom.net

1 3 5 4 2

Cover design by bigcheesedesign.com
Illustrations by Jon Berkeley
Origination by Currach Press
Printed by Nørhaven Book A/S, Denmark

ISBN 1-85607-932-5

Contents

Acknowledgements

I would like to acknowledge the efforts of the following individuals who, knowingly or unknowingly, aided and abetted in this book. These include James Dermot O'Flynn, Monica O'Flynn, John Egan, Denise O'Flynn, George and Anne Sisk, Maurice Blyth, Anna Barron, Mary Cotter, Margaret Bellew, Doreen Weafer, Jim Kilbride, Jim Dunne, Jimmy Woods (the only chef I knew who could burn water!), John Brennan of the Four Seasons Hotel Dublin (for educating my palate), Jim Bowe, Marie Brady, Lee Smith, John Roche, Prof. Ciaran O'Boyle, Paul Bokesberger, Oliver McMahon, Alison Speak, Uwe, Brendan Colclough, Desmond and Claire O'Flynn, Denise Lee, Amanda Chambers, Jenny Winter, Bairbre Stewart, Stephen Pearson, Catherine McBrinn, John Wilson, Marie-Jeanne Hedges, Brian Lynch, Simon Sleeman, and finally the great chefs including Eschofier, Constance Spry, Raymond Blanc, Keith Floyd, Gary Rhodes, Darina Allen and Jamie Oliver who have been an inspiration to me.

I am also indebted to the many clients and colleagues I have worked with over the years, which include Ashford Castle, Gresham Hotel, CERT, THF Hotels, the Burlington Hotel, Fáilte Ireland, Royal Marine Hotel, the

Irish Hotel & Catering Institute, Dublin College of Catering, Gulf Air, Vodafone, Eircell, Orange, Mater Private Hospital and the Royal College of Surgeons in Ireland.

And my final thanks go to my wife, Orla Fitzgerald, and my three children: Deirdre, Eimear and Dermot Jnr who never stopped encouraging me to have this book published.

Introduction

The concept of this book is to provide solutions to problems or potential problems that inevitably arise in the home kitchen.

Cooking is meant to be fun and enjoyable, however, too often it ends up a mess, particularly at party time! I have tried to identify – in a fun way – the crisis and the quick solution to the problem, so that an air of calm can be maintained in the kitchen at all times.

Kitchen Calm deliberately contain no recipes. Instead, it features tips and suggestions, and is small enough to fit into the pocket of a kitchen apron.

I have written this book because so many of my friends have asked me for cookery tips and solutions to simple cookery problems. I hope that this book will be a comfort to all in their kitchen.

Finally, anyone who would like to share their own pearls of wisdom can email me at kitchencalm@eircom.net.

General Tips

If you can read you can cook.

When following recipes, use only one set of measurements – do not mix metric and imperial.

Spoon measurements are always level. A tablespoon is 15ml and a teaspoon is 5ml.

When cooking with your partner for a dinner party always open a bottle of wine before you start. You will be amazed at the calming effect.

When using wine in a recipe, always use the best quality of wine that you can afford, as you will be able to enjoy drinking the other half of the bottle.

The secret to cooking success: preparation, preparation, preparation.

Wash all fresh produce before preparation.

Always check that you have the right ingredients before you start cooking. Check the quality of the ingredients. If in doubt throw it out.

Strong-smelling dry goods must be kept airtight or they lose their aroma. Coffee, herbs and spices all need special sealed containers.

Salt, flour and baking powder attract damp, so again, place them in sealed containers and if possible close to the cooker.

For emergencies, always carry 4 trays of ice in your fridge, you will read why!

Burnt the pot again? Put it into a sink of really cold water and then pour cold water into the pot. You will be amazed how easy the pot can be cleaned.

When you are running out of time do not try and boil the eggs in the microwave, unless you plan to clean the microwave for the rest of the week! My father made this mistake when he was learning to cook at age 65.

To cool a casserole dish or a dish cooked in a pot, quickly place in a sink full of cold water with the lid off and refresh the water in the sink every 5 minutes. Once cold, place in a fridge or freezer, thus preventing the growth of harmful bacteria.

Need two lemons for the recipe and only have one? Put the lemon into a hot oven for 4 minutes and you will get double the amount of lemon juice. You can do the same with oranges. Also if you have a microwave: 30 seconds at high will have the same result.

Too lazy to stir the milk when it's boiling? Just add a marble, as it will stir the milk for you. Remember though to remove the marble before serving.

To help you make really tasty gravy every time, always roast your meats on a bed of vegetables covered in water.

The gravy is all greasy – pour it hot through a cloth soaked in cold water and the grease will cling to the cloth. If you don't have a cloth throw a few ice cubes into the pot, the fat will cling to the ice cubes but make sure to remove them before they melt.

If you are lucky enough to receive a present of wild poultry and you have to pluck them, immerse the birds one at a time in boiling water for 1 minute. This makes the plucking easier and stops the feathers flying!

Want to slim while you eat? Marinate all your meat in lemon juice or good vinegar as the acids dissolve the animal fat. Don't forget to discard the marinade before cooking.

Squeeze lemon juice over cut apples, avocados, pears, bananas or mushrooms so that they don't go brown.

To be a success in the kitchen get yourself a good set of knives, a scissors and the ingredients listed in the chapter, 'What is required in the cupboard and fridge?'

Never allow meat, especially poultry, to make direct contact with the roasting tin. If you don't have a trivet, then use the tray from your grill pan. Put the bird sitting on this and make sure the oven is at the correct temperature.

To remove only the thinnest layers of rind from lemons or oranges, use your vegetable peeler: simple and effective.

The mayonnaise for the summer salad has just split or curdled. This can happen for many reasons: if the oil is added too quickly or is too cold, if the sauce is insufficiently whisked, or the yoke is stale and therefore weak.

The solution to the problem is to get a clean bowl, add a teaspoon of boiling water and gradually whisk in the curdled sauce.

Another solution is to take an egg yolk and whisk it with a half-teaspoon of water and then gradually whisk in the curdled sauce. The mayonnaise will now be perfect.

Keep it simple do not over-decorate food as it will look messed about and no longer appetising.

If you have to coat your meat with flour before cooking, place the pieces of meat in a paper or plastic bag, add the flour, then shake. This saves the mess. Seasoned flour is often used in recipes, so for every 200g/8oz of flour add 1 level teaspoon of salt and a half-teaspoon of ground black pepper.

Before carving a roasted bird, allow it to stand for 20 mins covered with a warm damp cloth or foil. This allows the flesh to relax and makes carving much easier.

Over the last year I have been to two dinner parties where the host has asked me to rescue the hollandaise sauce. The main reason hollandaise sauce curdles is that the melted butter has been added too quickly, or the sauce has been heated excessively and the eggs start to harden, shrink and separate from the liquid i.e. become scrambled. The simple solution is to get a new bowl, pour in a teaspoon of boiling water and gradually whisk in the curdled sauce.

Always heat your oven before using, so that the whole of the oven reaches the appropriate temperature for your dish.

Oven temperatures:

Centigrade	Farenheight	Gas
70	150	¼
80	175	¼
100	200	½
110	225	½
130	250	1
140	275	1
150	300	2
170	325	3
180	350	4
190	375	5
200	400	6
220	425	7
230	450	8
240	475	8
250	500	9
270	525	9
290	550	9

Weights conversion, grams to ounces:

Grams	Ounces
25g	1oz
50g	2oz
75g	3oz
100g	4oz
200g	8oz
300g	12oz
400g	16oz

If boiling an egg always time from when the water starts to boil. Large egg soft-boiled: 3minutes, medium egg soft-boiled: 2.5 minutes. Large egg hard-boiled 10 minutes, medium egg hard-boiled:
9 minutes.

To chop fresh herbs don't chop with a knife
– use a scissors instead.

For perfect back rashers and no mess, place
the rasher on a tin foil-covered baking tray in
a preheated oven at 180°C/350°F/gas 4. Cook
for 7 minutes and then turn and cook for
another 3 minutes. The bacon will be flat and
perfect every time. You can do the same with
sausages, but they need to be pricked with a
fork and cooked for about 20 minutes or
until brown.

Keep it fresh: sprigs of fresh herbs used for
garnish should always be absolutely fresh.

If you like your steak well done without drying it out, cook it to medium and finish it off for 3-5 minutes in the microwave oven. This also works with duck and lamb, as the microwave cooks from the inside out.

Cook new potatoes in boiling water, old potatoes should be started in cold water.

Root vegetables should be cooked in cold water, while all other vegetables should be cooked in boiling water.

To stop vegetables boiling over add a small bit of butter or cooking oil.

Root vegetables should be cooked in cold water, while all other vegetables should be cooked in boiling water.

If possible vegetables should be steamed or microwaved, thus reducing the loss of natural vitamins and minerals.

Add a new flavour to your fresh potato soup by adding a teaspoon of pesto to each bowl before serving.

Always throw salt into boiling water, as it stains the pot blue if you put the salt into cold water.

To keep your homemade croutons fresh, place them in a sealed jar or plastic bag in the fridge.

For lighter pancakes or crepes make them with cold water instead of milk and stand the batter for 1 hour before cooking.

For perfect rice every time boil a large saucepan of water, then put in 2 cups of basmati or long grain rice. Bring back to the boil and simmer for 8 minutes. Strain and rinse under hot water tap. Transfer to an ovenproof dish and place in a warm oven at 180°C/350°F/gas 4 for 5 minutes. Before serving, fluff with a fork.

An alternative is to cook the rice in a hot oven at 180°C/350°F/gas 4, by placing 2 cupfuls of rice into a lidded Pyrex dish with 5 cups of boiling water. Add salt to taste and allow to cook for half an hour.

To thicken sauce naturally, keep some home cooked roux in a screw top jar in the fridge and when required, whisk in a little at a time to the sauce you want to thicken. Then boil for a minute to cook the flour.

Cutting rashers or bacon is easier with a scissors.

If cooking risotto, Arborio rice is best, as it gives a nice creamy texture when finished.

Long, slow cooking tenderises meat and develops a wonderful flavour in stews and casseroles.

Use a wooden spoon to sauté as it doesn't get too hot and is safer. Also it won't mark your non-stick saucepan and frying pan.

Always cook mince quickly and thoroughly. There must be no trace of pink as it can cause food poisoning.

When cooking savoury mince experiment by trying minced beef, pork, lamb, chicken and turkey.

When using soya sauce, use light soya sauce with chicken and fish dishes, and dark soya sauce with beef and lamb.

If using tinned tomatoes in a recipe, use unflavoured tomatoes as the flavour is more authentic.

When making stuffing for pork or chicken, try some dried tarragon for a change.

Chicken should be washed before use and dried in kitchen paper. It should be cooked quickly and thoroughly with no pink in the flesh and no juice running. If using a temperature probe, the internal temperature should be 80°C/175°F/gas ¼.

A stew boiled is a stew spoiled.

Never salt the surface of meat before grilling or barbecuing as salt draws out the juices and the meat will not brown well. Brush meat with olive oil before cooking to protect it.

Desserts and Baking

The secret to successful pastry-making is having everything cold. Cold hands, cold fat, cold water and cold rolling surface. My cookery teacher in college said I would never make good pastry as my hands were too warm. She was right.

When rolling pastry, always sprinkle flour on your rolling surface and rolling pin but never directly on to the pastry.

The secret to successful pastry-making is having everything cold. Cold hands, cold fat, cold water and cold rolling surface.

The reason for chilling pastry in the fridge for half an hour before cooking is that it will prevent shrinking when cooked.

Always keep a small plastic bag beside you when making pastry, so that if the phone rings you can slip your hand into the bag and answer the phone. Alternatively put the answering machine on or divert your calls to voicemail.

If using dry fruit for baking, soak it in hot water to allow it to soften and swell, then dry it carefully on a cloth in a dry place.

If you use wet fruit when baking, your cake will sink.

When stewing apples, add a squeeze of lemon juice to keep them nice and white

To beat egg whites successfully, the bowl and whisk must be grease-free. Eggs must be separated properly and there must be no yolk in the whites.

When making bread and butter pudding, why not be trendy by using croissant or barm brack?

When bread is properly cooked, there should be a hollow sound underneath when tapped.

To check that your cake is cooked, insert a skewer and it should come out dry.

A cooked sponge should spring back when lightly pressed with your finger.

When baking, non-stick tins are the best to use, as there is no need to grease them. Other tins are best greased with white fat e.g. Flora, margarine.

If you don't have a baking sheet, go out and buy one!

No buttermilk for the brown bread? Don't panic. Use fresh milk and add a tablespoon of white vinegar or lemon juice, or use fresh milk and add a heaped teaspoon cream of tarter to the flour.

When cooking a large tart or flan, preheat a baking sheet in the oven and then place the Pyrex dish on top of it. This helps to crisp the bottom of large tarts.

When making profiteroles always use small eggs as this will keep the pastry light

Scone dough can be used as a pizza base by omitting the caster sugar.

When making mince pies for Christmas, why not grate a cooking apple into your mince? It makes a nice change.

To apply a pretty pattern to a sponge cake, place a doyley on top of the sponge cake and sieve icing sugar over it. Then carefully lift off the doyley. For a chocolate sponge you can sieve a mixture of cocoa and icing sugar on top.

If using self-raising flour in your recipe, omit the baking powder.

When making coffee icing for cakes use Irel instead of instant coffee.

When making biscuits, butter gives the best flavour, so don't use substitutes.

To ensure biscuits cook evenly, turn the tin once during baking.

When cooked, biscuits should be soft to touch, but will harden on cooling.

Always store your biscuits in an airtight tin.

Microwave Cooking

Only use suitable dishes for microwave cooking e.g. Pyrex.

To cook evenly, cut food into equal size portions.

Place the thickest parts of foods at the outer edge of the dish so that they are exposed to more microwaves.

Arrange food to be cooked in a circle.

To prevent bursting, pierce all foods that have skins, e.g. apples, tomatoes, jacket potatoes.

Score whole fish with your filleting knife as this prevents bursting.

Where possible cover food as it will cook quicker.

The type of wattage of a microwave cooker can mean the difference of plus or minus 2-3 minutes in cooking times. So always test your food to make sure it is cooked

Turn foods that are more then 2cm thick

Food with a high sugar or fat content can burn easily in the microwave. You have been warned!

When cooking food in a microwave, standing time is a necessity not an option. Food needs to rest for a while to allow cooking to complete.

If you have too many fresh herbs, dry them in the microwave by placing them between sheets of kitchen paper on the turntable for 3-5 minutes at medium.

If honey has crystallised, place it in a bowl and hit high for 30 seconds at a time until it becomes runny. Look at it every 30 seconds as it can burn easily.

To toast almonds place them on a plate with a knob of butter and heat at high for 3-4 minutes. Stir every minute until golden brown.

To soften cream cheese place the cheese on a plate unwrapped and heat on low for 1 minute.

Chocolate can be melted in the microwave as long as you add 2 teaspoons of milk and be careful not to burn it.

To peel garlic easily, place the garlic cloves in the microwave and cook on high for 30-40 seconds. Squeeze the garlic at one end and garlic cloves pop out.

To peel garlic easily, place the garlic cloves in the microwave and cook on high for 30-40 seconds. Squeeze the garlic at one end and garlic cloves pop out.

To clean your microwave naturally, just place a cut lemon in a bowl with an inch of water and microwave for 5 minutes at high. When finished just wipe with a cloth.

Pre-dinner Party Tips

If you don't have time to clean the house yourself before the party, book the cleaning fairies for 3 hours, it is will be worth it.

Flowers, soft lighting and music all set the scene for a great evening. If the mood is right nobody will notice the cracks in the wall.

If trying out new dishes for your party, test them on your family or close friends first.

The most successful hosts are those who are relaxed. Have you ever been to a dinner party where the host is all uptight?

Be ready to greet your guests as they arrive. A warm welcome from the host/hostess gets things off to a good start.

Small informal groups tend to mix much quicker if you introduce correctly and let them help themselves to drinks.

Finger food should be finger food, so don't serve awkward, soggy drippy food, unless you want to clean up for the rest of the week and pay your guests' dry cleaning bills.

If serving hors d'oeuvres before dinner arrange them on separate plates. Your guest will be able to identify what's on the plate without interrupting a lively discussion.

Invest in a dozen good glasses, as lovely glasses make the drink and the person holding it look much better.

Drinks before dinner should last no longer then 45 minutes. Endless drinks result in bored guests or guests who have drunk so much that they ignore the food and cause other problems.

If serving hors d'oeuvres before dinner arrange them on separate plates. Your guest will be able to identify what's on the plate without interrupting a lively discussion.

Forgot to chill the white wine for the fish starter? Just empty 2 trays of ice into a jug. Pour the white wine into the jug, stir gently for 2 minutes and pour the wine back into the bottle. Serve immediately and put another bottle in the freezer.

Make your life easy and enjoy the party more by having a cold starter or soup, followed by a hot main course and a cold dessert. Remember don't try and do hot soufflé for 8. They rarely rise under pressure and you will feel deflated.

Cook meat in batches of not more then 20 portions, as it is difficult to cook it thoroughly in larger amounts.

Allow yourself 30 minutes to unwind before your guests arrive. Have one good drink and then confine yourself to sipping until the main course is served.

My father tells a story of a doctor's wife who loved entertaining. On one occasion, however, she had more then one stiff drink before the guests arrived and subsequently collapsed over the sofa. Luckily she wasn't hurt. The male guest had to carry her up to bed while the females in the party tried to figure out what was cooking in the kitchen. Once everything was sorted a great night was had by all.

Plan the menu so that the dishes can be prepared in advance and avoid repetition of ingredients.

Serve hot food on really hot plates and cold food on cold plates. Simple, but people forget to do this all the time

Offer your guest hot freshen-up towels after the main course. Dampened towels take 30 seconds to heat in the microwave.

Do not overload the plate, but take the time to arrange things neatly and attractively.

The side of the steak, chicken breast or lamb cutlet cooked first looks best, so always serve this side up.

Over-decorated food often looks messed about and no longer appetising. The more cluttered the plate, the less attractive it inevitably it becomes.

If plating the main course keep it simple and relevant by using the right garnish. A garnish of dill goes with salmon. A sprig of watercress complements lamb cutlets nicely by giving it texture, taste and colour. Sprinkling parsley over everything, however, just makes a mess.

Always prepare your garnishes in advance, so that hot food does not go cold.

If serving cheese, remember to take it out of its wrappers early and serve at room temperature. Always serve the cheese with good quality crackers or French stick.

Individual tarts, puddings, etc. look better for presentation and are easier to plate. Furthermore, portion control becomes easier and avoids leaving yourself short.

Avoid cooking too many vegetables. One or two vegetables cooked correctly, is an awful lot better then 4 or 5 soggy cold ones.

Portion Control

Basic guide to portion control per person:

Soup allow 150ml/5fl oz per person.

Meat off the bone: 100-112g/4oz per person.

Meat on the bone: 150-180g/6oz per person.

Fish: 100-112g/4oz per person.

Portion of potatoes: 100-112g/4oz per person.

Vegetables: 100-112g/4oz per person.

For desserts allow 1.5 portions per person. This allows for seconds and guests who want to try more the one.

If serving cheese allow 3oz per person.

Advance planning allows you prepare enough, but not too much, food for your guests.

Food Safety or How to Keep the Bugs at Bay

Kitchen bugs like moisture and warmth, so don't give them these ideal conditions.

Place raw meat at the bottom of your fridge. This ensures that no blood drips on to food in the fridge.

Your fridge temperature should be at a constant 4°C.

Kitchen bugs like moisture and warmth, so don't give them these ideal conditions.

Always place raw meat on a plate with a lip and wrap it in peach paper as this prevents reduction in moisture of the meat.

Wrap food loosely and let it breathe.

Never store raw and cooked foods together.

Always thaw out your poultry before cooking. This reduces the risk of salmonella.

If you have made a fresh mayonnaise, eat it as soon as possible or place it in the fridge.

Keep your cooking utensils clean at all time, and change your tea towels and j-cloths daily.

Barbecues

Never pierce the skin of meat or fish when turning it on the barbecue as you will lose the savoury juices on the surface of the meat. Always use good thongs to turn the food.

If using wooden skewers for kebabs, always soak the skewers in water beforehand.

Always have a sprinkling bottle of water, as you will need to control the flames.

Avoid barbecues that dip in the centre, as the food will burn.

For a quick and effective barbecue, just take the grill tray from the oven and place it on top of two bricks.

Never use ordinary firelighters, petrol or paraffin, as they can flare and give a bad flavour to the food.

If you are using charcoal always place some aluminium foil – reflective side up – underneath the coals. The foil causes the heat to be thrown back against the grill and makes it easier to gather up the ashes afterwards.

Marinating meat before barbecuing adds flavour and will tenderise cheaper cuts. If meat has not been marinated, baste it with olive oil and season. Marinade mixtures can also be used as bastes.

The barbecue is ready when a thin layer of grey ash covers the coals. This takes about 30-40 minutes depending on how thick the layer of charcoal is.

If you have difficulty lighting the charcoal, place it in an old roasting tin and put the tin in a hot oven for 30 minutes. Then transfer back to the barbecue. Within minutes the charcoal will glow and be ready for cooking.

The barbecue is ready when a thin layer of grey ash covers the coals. This takes about 30-40 minutes depending on how thick the layer of charcoal is.

Never start grilling if there are still flames, as
the food will burn on the outside and be raw
on the inside.

To increase the temperature of the barbecue:
lift the grill, move the coals to the centre, tap
off the extra ash and lower the barbecue grill
again.

To decrease the temperature of the
barbecue, close the grill vents, spread the
coals out and raise the height of the grill.

Before you start cooking, lightly grease the
barbecue grill, as this prevents the meat
sticking.

Trim all meat of excess fat, as this will prevent the fat causing the fire to flame. The remaining fat should be snipped in several places with a scissors to prevent the edges of the meat from curling up.

When barbecuing fish, use a sandwich grip for grilling small fish and a fish-shaped grip for larger fish.

Pre-cooking chicken for 15 minutes in an oven before placing on the barbecue, can prevent the risk of serving undercooked meat and also keeps the meat from drying out.

General rule to barbecue cooking times:

Fish: 5-10 minutes with flesh scored

Steak: 5-8 minutes each side

Pork chops: 12-18 minutes

Lamb chops: 5-10 minutes

Burgers: 10-15 minutes

Chicken portions on the bone: 30 minutes

Chicken breast: 20-25 minutes

Meat kebabs: 10-20 minutes

If the weather changes on the day make sure you have a make-shift canvas cover or a large umbrella. You can always cook out and eat in.

Make sure you have a good bristle brush. Avoid nylon or plastic ones, as they tend to melt.

Salads

Salads delight the palate and excite the eye.
Suddenly the most ordinary foods combined
to complement each other in colour, texture
and shape become works of art.

Oak lettuce and lollo rossa lettuce wilt
quickly and often look unusable. However
they can be revived by submerging in a large
bowl of very cold water for 40 minutes
before use.

Never drown your salad: place the dressing in the base of the salad bowl, with layers of salad leaves on top. Toss at the table before serving.

If you have no vinegar in the house to make salad dressing, you can always use lemon juice instead.

If you have to skin tomatoes for your salad, put each tomato on a slotted spoon into boiling water and count to six. Remove from the water and plunge into a bowl of iced water to stop the cooking. The skin should peel off easily without tearing the flesh, which should be still smooth and firm.

If you have to skin tomatoes for your salad, put each tomato on a slotted spoon into boiling water and count to six.

When serving salad leaves as part of a main course allow 50-85g/2-3oz per person.

When tossing salads use a bowl about 4 times larger then the volume of leaves. This makes mixing, tossing and dressing much easier and gives better results.

Only toss salad leaves in their dressing, minutes before serving, otherwise they will wilt and will lose their crisp texture and fresh appearance.

Salads of root vegetables, grains and pulses will improve in flavour if dressed several hours before serving.

Christmas Dinner

Christmas dinner is the easiest dinner to prepare. However, people over-complicate it and get very stressed. To enjoy a stress-free Christmas do the following:

Make your stuffing, cook your ham and prepare your vegetables on Christmas Eve.

Only cook two vegetables and do one stuffing.

*Before putting the turkey in the oven, make sure you have
heated the oven to the required temperature.*

If possible set your table the night before and don't forget to chill your white wine and champagne.

Before putting the turkey in the oven, make sure you have heated the oven to the required temperature.

To test if the turkey is cooked, just turn both legs. They should turn with no resistance and the juices between the legs should run clearly.

Having stuffed the turkey or chicken, sew it up using dental floss or use a stainless steel poultry lacer – a magic piece of equipment.

For moister turkey breasts, cook the turkey upside down.

For a moist turkey and a clean oven, cook the turkey in a cook bag.

To light the Christmas pudding, gently warm a silver spoon over a candle. When warm pour some brandy onto the spoon and return over the heat of the candle. After about a minute the brandy will ignite with a blue flame, which you can now pour over the Christmas pudding.

Turkey cooking time: 15 minutes per 1lb/454g and 30 minutes over at 180°C/350°F/gas 4.

Fish

Fresh fish should smell of seawater and not of fish. The eyes should be bright – almost alert – and the gills bright red.

When buying fish don't be afraid to prod and poke. Also remember that the fish should be firm and tight, not soggy and flaky.

Always get your fishmonger to clean and fillet your fish.

Never buy pre-cooked shellfish, especially lobster or crayfish. They should be alive and kicking and they should feel heavy and dense.

We used to go on summer holidays to Donabate in north County Dublin and, fortnightly, a patient of my fathers used to arrive at the house with 2 large lobsters. He would go into the kitchen, place the lobsters in a large pot of cold water, and he would not leave until he had a glass of whiskey and the lobsters were cooked. I can still taste those lobster. They were amazing!

Always plan a fish meal and order your fish in advance, then plan on how you are going to cook it.

If you are lucky enough to get a gift of freshly-caught fish and don't know how to prepare it, here is what to do. Cut off all the fins using a scissors. Scale the fish by running a blunt knife from the tail to the head. Slit open the belly and remove the intestines. Some fish, like trout, have a blood sac running along the backbone, so scrape this out with the point of your knife. Rinse well under cold water and pat dry the fish. Cook the fish as soon as possible as there is nothing nicer then fresh fish straight from the sea

Essential utensils for preparing and cooking fish include filleting knife, scissors and a blunt knife for scaling.

When filleting a large round fish (e.g. mackerel, cod, trout or salmon) make a vertical incision behind the head until you reach the bone, then turn the knife on its side and run it along the bone to the tail. Always sharpen your filleting knife before you do this.

If you want to fillet a flat fish (e.g. sole or plaice), run a sharp knife along the central line on one side. Lay the knife sideways to the bone and slice to the edge and the tail, at the same time lifting the fillet free with your other hand.

A knob of savoury butter will cheer up the simplest piece of fish.

Fresh fish should smell of seawater and not of fish. The eyes should be bright – almost alert – and the gills bright red.

When serving sauce with fish, don't swamp
the fish: 3-4 tablespoons per person will be
sufficient

For perfect whole salmon, wrap the salmon
in tinfoil with some wine, butter and fresh
herbs. Cook until the skin comes away easily.
Do not overcook.

What's Required in the Cupboard and Fridge?

The basics are extra virgin olive oil, sunflower oil, balsamic vinegar, white wine vinegar, whole grain mustard, Dijon mustard, mustard powder, table salt, sea salt, black pepper corns, milled black pepper, brown sugar, white sugar, icing sugar, self-raising flour, plain flour, baking soda, basmati rice, long grain rice, pasta of all shapes and sizes, couscous, black olives, green olives, soya sauce, tereyaki sauce, tomato puree, tinned tomatoes, cocoa powder, Bournville chocolate, cloves, nutmeg, dried basil, oregano, herbs de provence, sundried tomatoes, jam and marmalade.

The Fridge:
Cream, butter, free range eggs, rashers, cheddar cheese, Parmesan cheese and orange juice.

Fresh Things:
Fresh stuff is perishable, however, you should always have apples, oranges, lemons, bananas, onions, spring onions, carrots, broccoli, potatoes, fresh herbs and mangetout.

There are certain things you should always have in your kitchen.

Notes

Notes

Notes

Notes

Notes